Lyons, John B.
Oliver St. John Gogarty

Oliver St. John Gogarty

THE IRISH WRITERS SERIES
James F. Carens, General Editor

EIMAR O'DUFFY	Robert Hogan
J. C. MANGAN	James Kilroy
J. M. SYNGE	Robin Skelton
PAUL VINCENT CARROLL	Paul A. Doyle
SEAN O'CASEY	Bernard Benstock
SEUMAS O'KELLY	George Brandon Saul
SHERIDAN LEFANU	Michael Begnal
SOMERVILLE AND ROSS	John Cronin
STANDISH O'GRADY	Phillip L. Marcus
SUSAN L. MITCHELL	Richard M. Kain
W. R. RODGERS	Darcy O'Brien
MERVYN WALL	Robert Hogan
LADY GREGORY	Hazard Adams
LIAM O'FLAHERTY	James O'Brien
MARIA EDGEWORTH	James Newcomer
SIR SAMUEL FERGUSON	Malcolm Brown
BRIAN FRIEL	D. E. S. Maxwell
PEADAR O'DONNELL	Grattan Freyer
DANIEL CORKERY	George Brandon Saul
BENEDICT KIELY	Daniel Casey
CHARLES ROBERT MATURIN	Robert E. Lougy
DOUGLAS HYDE	Gareth Dunleavy
EDNA O'BRIEN	Grace Eckley
FRANCIS STUART	J. H. Natterstad
JOHN BUTLER YEATS	Douglas N. Archibald
JOHN MONTAGUE	Frank Kersnowski
KATHARINE TYNAN	Marilyn Gaddis Rose
BRIAN MOORE	Jeanne Flood
PATRICK KAVANAGH	Darcy O'Brien
OLIVER ST. JOHN GOGARTY	J. B. Lyons
GEORGE FITZMAURICE	Arthur McGuinness

GEORGE RUSSELL (AE)	Richard M. Kain and James H. O'Brien
IRIS MURDOCH	Donna Gerstenberger
MARY LAVIN	Zack Bowen
FRANK O'CONNOR	James H. Matthews
ELIZABETH BOWEN	Edwin J. Kenney, Jr.
WILLIAM ALLINGHAM	Alan Warner
SEAMUS HEANEY	Robert Buttel
THOMAS DAVIS	Eileen Sullivan

OLIVER
ST. JOHN GOGARTY

J. B. Lyons

Lewisburg
BUCKNELL UNIVERSITY PRESS
London: Associated University Presses

©1976 by Associated University Presses, Inc.

Associated University Presses, Inc.
Cranbury, New Jersey 08512

Associated University Presses
108 New Bond Street
London W1Y OQX, England

Library of Congress Cataloging in Publication Data

Lyons, John Benignus.
  Oliver St. John Gogarty.

  (The Irish writers series)
  Bibliography: p.
  1. Gogarty, Oliver St. John, 1878-1957.
PR6013.028Z75   821'.9'12   73-8260
ISBN 0-8387-1359-9
ISBN 0-8387-1397-1 pbk.

Printed in the United States of America

Contents

Preface

In an unpublished poem, "The Changeling," Oliver St. John Gogarty declared

> They ought to have guarded my cradle better
> In Number Five Rutland Square, East;
> In Dublin they thought it need not be done;
> My Father was talking about his prize setter,
> My Mother preparing my baptismal feast,
> When who should slip in but a fairy from Letter
> (My nurse saw him dodging that day through the town)
> Who softly undid each invisible fetter
> That bound me to monarch, to lawyer, to priest,
> To Father and Mother and kin of my own,
> I'm no better off by becoming the debtor
> Forever, and ever the Good People's guest,
> And from my own kindred aloof and alone.

His diagnosis of an anarchic personality was accurate but, a gregarious man, he was never aloof and rarely alone. His literary career falls into three periods: in the first his days seesawed between exquisite lyricism and the protective obscenity of medical student life; the second, despite an assured professional position with attendant responsibilities, saw a considerable output of prose and verse; the third, in America, lacking the day-to-day stimuli of his native environment, was the least successful.

Latterly there has been a tendency to neglect, and even to denigrate Gogarty, but the action of a small group of medical students who in 1971 established an "Oliver Gogarty Society" and placed a plaque on his birthplace may be an indication that his period in that literary purgatory into which so many dead authors are thrust by living critics is ending. If so, it is opportune to suggest (mixing Christian and pagan ideas) that if his place on Mount Olympus is ready a note of this should be published.

His position on those happy slopes is debatable—there is room at the top even there—and presumably it will be debated with increasing frequency as we approach his centenary year. Meanwhile, two Dubliners who did him honor may be cited. William Doolin, an erudite medical editor, called Gogarty the last of Ireland's "Wild Geese" and prophesied that his lyrics would be remembered "so long as there are men to quote them." Myles na Gopaleen in his column in the *Irish Times*—"a corner often used for derision"—expressed in measured words his admiration for "this great man."

In accordance with the format of the Series, my account of Gogarty is neccessarily brief and, space being precious, I hope that the librarians and other individuals who helped me will accept my thanks collectively. I must, however, make special mention of Mr. Oliver D. Gogarty, S.C., and his sister Mrs. Brenda Williams for granting access to their father's papers. Permission to quote from the *Collected Poems* has been granted by the Devin-Adair Company, New York City.

Chronology

1878	Born August 17 in Dublin.
1896	Enters Royal University.
1898	Transfers to School of Physic, Dublin University.
1902-3-5	Wins Vice-Chancellor's Prize for Verse.
1904	Spends two terms at Worcester College, Oxford.
1906	Marries Martha Duane.
1907	Obtains medical degree.
1908	Commences practice in ear-nose-and-throat surgery.
1910	Takes Fellowship of Royal College of Surgeons in Ireland.
1911	Appointment as ENT Surgeon to Meath Hospital.
1916	*Hyperthuleana* published.
1917	Purchases Renvyle House.
	Opening night of *Blight* at Abbey Theatre December 11.
1919	Opening nights of *A Serious Thing* and *The Enchanted Trousers.*
1922	Member of Irish Free State Senate.

1923   Attempted assassination on January 19.
        Renvyle House burned down on February 19.
        Transfers practice temporarily to London.
1924   Returns to Dublin; presents swans to Liffey; *An Offering of Swans* wins Tailteann Medal.
1930   Renvyle House opened as hotel.
1932   Foundation member of Irish Academy of Letters.
1937   *As I Was Going Down Sackville Street* published.
1938   *I Follow St. Patrick* published.
1939   *Tumbling in the Hay* published; goes to America.
1957   September 19, heart attack in New York City, dies September 22.

Oliver St. John Gogarty

1

As a Young Man

From Parnell Square (formerly Rutland Square) Dublin to Renvyle on the Atlantic fringe is a four-hours' drive in a fast car, a slightly shorter space of time than a jet plane takes to span the Atlantic Ocean to New York from Shannon. Seventy years ago, in Oliver St. John Gogarty's youth, these cardinal points in his life—born in 5 Rutland Square on August 17, 1878, he died in Manhattan and meanwhile Connemara had afforded many idle happy days—seemed set at greater distances. More distinctly, too, than today's "world-besotted traveller" might see them they reflect different aspects of Gogarty's many-faceted personality. Dublin, where wit is prized above riches, was his native background; at its shores lie the golden strands of Merrion and Portmarnock and behind the city the hills which James Stephens said were conceived by God and sculptured by Praxiteles. Connemara, unimaginably beautiful, appealed irresistibly to the fastidious mind behind the masks imposed by circumstances. New York City and the American continent eventually offered reentry to a

belated *vie de Bohème* where professional cares ceased
and the promise of rewards and literary acclaim beck-
oned.

He was the eldest son of Dr. Henry Gogarty, FRCSI
(Fellow of the Royal College of Surgeons in Ireland),
and his wife, Margaret Oliver, the daughter of a
prosperous Galway miller. He was born with a caul and
the traditional good fortune accompanying that event
took the form of robust health and an optimistic
temperament.

His parents were well-to-do. In addition to their
commodious house in fashionable Rutland Square they
owned Fairfield, a countryhouse a short distance from
the city. Its garden was sheltered to the north and west
by yews, its east wall covered with cherry trees. Here in
summertime, when young Oliver tired of playing, there
were linnets and finches and blackbirds to watch, and
here in this rose-scented garden his lyric sense was
nurtured. To Fairfield and to Kilbeg in County Meath
(owned by his father's friend Farrell O'Reilly) he owed
a soul "that is made of waters, fields and trees, with a
background of fairyland not too far away."

His first school was the Christian Brothers' School,
North Richmond Street. "They were the best educators
in the country," he recalled in *It Isn't That Time of
Year at All*! "and that is why my father sent me there."
This parent's death from appendicitis in 1891 does not
appear to have left the family in straitened circum-
stances, but for Oliver, who was sent to a succession of
boarding schools—Mungret College near Limerick,
Stonyhurst in England, and finally Clongowes in County
Kildare—it brought "a change to misery and servitude."

Not a boy, however, to languish in unhappiness, he displayed considerable athletic prowess. While still a schoolboy he played soccer for Preston and for Bohemians; he was a strong swimmer and became a champion cyclist.

Dr. Henry Gogarty's father and grandfather had been medical practitioners and his son hardly bothered to consider any alternative to a medical career. He entered the Royal University in 1896 but, if the account given in *Tumbling in the Hay* is to be credited, his mother was offended by the Registrar's brusqueness when she visited the Catholic University Medical School in Cecilia Street and transferred Oliver forthwith to Trinity College where her late husband had graduated. Be that as it may, the consequence was that by his acquaintance with both the Royal and Trinity he enjoyed the best (of the former some would say the *worst*) of both worlds: Barney, Weary, the four Halogens, John Elwood and, of course, James Augustine Joyce, were students of the Royal with whom Gogarty drank in Golly's pub in Fownes' Street and adventured to Nighttown; Mahaffy, Macran, and Tyrrell were Trinity dons with whom Gogarty took sherry in more exalted surroundings.

He astounded the middle-aged academics. Tales of his outrageous pranks reached their ears and their wide-opened eyes took stock of a gladiator's physique ideally balanced by a sensitive mind, the whole nicely salted with wit. With well-mannered humor he took their drinks and their patronage. In time they were to be his friends; Mahaffy would stay with him in the west and admire the plum-colored hills, but of the dons his dearest friend was to be "our graius homo" Robert Yelverton Tyrrell with his "iambic walk and Periclean smile."

> You shared with us the mood serene
> That ruled the universal scene
> When Peace was guardian of the poor,
> And only rusty was the door
> Of Janus, and the pillared shade
> Revealed the studious colonnade:
> The toga with the purple hem,
> The temple that with quiet flame
> Acclaimed the distant Emperor,
> Aternae lucis Redditor.

In his early years at Trinity, anatomy, which he had difficulty in memorizing, was his *bête noire*; cycling his chief physical preoccupation; poetry, which he memorized effortlessly, his intellectual joy. The verses of his own composition of that period which gained widest circulation were those which featured the obscene, of which the following parody of Yeats's "The Pity of Love" is a good example:

> A pity beyond all telling
> Is hid in the heart of love
> As soon as your penis is well in
> As soon as you give it a shove
> In the house where the whores are dwelling
> —Unless it is wrapped in a glove—
> A little Hunterian swelling
> Poxes the part that they love.

But behind the mask of "the smutster and funster" which, as he was aware, typified him in the eyes of

many, a serious mind was expressing itself in stanzas of
growing sensitivity, some of which were published in
Dana and elsewhere, and others, such as the following
tender love lyric, which remained uncollected:

Powder your neck lest there be seen
The marks where kissing lips have been.
But have a care the powder be
Matched to your round neck's ivorie
Lest by the difference of hue
Suspicion fall on me and you.

The sport which Gogarty found the most exhilarating
was cycling. Among the hardened semi-professionals
who raced for prizes to sell, his limbs were tested to the
utmost; his mind had to be alert to the dangers of spills,
accidental or contrived. He wore red custom-made
cycling shoes with special blocks for the pedals and a
personally designed jersey, but however dandified he
looked he was in every way a match for the toughest
contenders.

At Ballinafeigh in County Antrim when he was
taking the lead, an opponent tried to force him against
the curb. Gogarty spread his elbows in self-defense. "As
I was about to be killed his handle-bar hit my elbow and
he changed his mind as suddenly as his direction . . ."

Within the sporting confines of College Park a cyclist
could be more reflective. Circling the grass track,
Gogarty was amused by the realization that he was
speeding on *Poa pratensis*. And the fledgling botanist
who recalled Linnaeus as "the bird who knelt down and
praised God when he saw a gorse bush in bloom"

disliked the realities which his mentors disclosed. The scent of new-mown grass gave up its secret—coumarin. How debasing! The essence of summer reduced to a chemical formula!

As he circled, he tells us in *Tumbling in the Hay*, he was watched disapprovingly—or so he thought, indulging undergraduate persecutory sentiments—by a pipe-smoking anatomist who plowed him repeatedly in the anatomy examination. Perhaps it was just as well, then, that the Amateur Athletic Association suspended him for bad language during a race in the Phoenix Park, for if this did nothing to increase his interest in anatomy it did leave him free to cultivate his literary interests.

His literary career was influenced, too, by W. B. Yeats whom he met in the Nassau Hotel in 1902 and with whom his relationship was at first that of an irreverent disciple, later a sincere but sometimes mocking friend.

Gogarty spent the Hilary and Trinity terms of 1904 at Worcester College, Oxford, hoping to win the Newdigate Prize for verse; but he came second. The prize went to G. K. A. Bell, with whom he became friendly. In July he informed Bell that he would soon move into a Martello Tower he had rented in Sandy-cove—"I shall thence send many lines to thee."

His correspondence with Bell is a remarkable contrast to that with Joyce. When both are read, opposite sides of Gogarty's personality, kind but malicious, lyrical but salacious, are disclosed. He is at his best with Bell and not merely on his best behavior—not even for the future Bishop of Chichester does he completely eschew blasphemy—but displaying his finer qualities. One gathers that his overflowing energy ("I arose at 3.30 and saw the dawn") made his letter-writing effortless and artless, the latter only in the sense that he uses no art to conceal but tells his friend what he has been up to—buying a live lobster to set it free! "My lobster is now wandering in the weird submarine moonlight which they say is visible night and day by the amimalculae at the sea-bottom and stretching his stiffened joints and (if he could) wondering had he been to Hades and gained a rebirth"—or courting a girl on the Hill of Howth: "I lay under a rhododendron and watched the midges dance like a fountain for joy of the sunlight. I mixed light purple rhododendron leaves in a girl's red brown hair."

The letters to Bell throw new light on Gogarty's character, revealing unexpected moments of melancholy, a slight disaffection towards a medical career, and little or nothing of the mockery of himself and others which is a feature of his correspondence with Joyce.

> There are moments when 'my stillest hour' takes possession of me, moments invariably sad. Sadness is fundamental with us, let it be nobly borne. It is unbecoming to let it degenerate into misery . . . .

Writing from the Martello Tower in August 1904 he described for Bell the splendid view of Howth to the north and the wonderful succession of colors. "Pink on a hot and sunny day. Purple or cerulean on clouded days." The unusual adjective recently led a reviewer in the *Times Literary Supplement* to conclude that Gogarty had in mind Sir Samuel Ferguson's "silent, cerulean-skirted showers," but cerulean occurs in the terminology of anatomy and pathology, *locus caeruleus* and *morbus caeruleus*, and would have been a familiar word to a medical student.

When medicine palled on bright summer days his thoughts instinctively turned to literature, but his textbooks were not neglected through indolence but because of more attractive reading; the pages of Santayana, Emerson, Arnold, Mahaffy and Jebb interested him more than Osler's *Principles and Practice of Medicine*.

His article "The Irish Literary Revival" was published in the *Evening Mail* on March 4, 1905, and drew attention to lack of critical standards concerning literary merit, confusion about what makes literature national, and disagreement about the conception of drama. "We are content to compare and not to criticise, with the result that when confronted with any form of art to which we cannot immediately apply a precedent we are puzzled."

As an example he cited the failure of the public to appreciate the Irish National Literary Theatre's performance of Yeats's *The Shadowy Waters* because it had neither action nor crisis—because it was not dramatic. He himself, on the other hand, knowing that no claim had been made for the dramatic excellence of the piece, enjoyed it: he had found it "a new and charming form of art—a lyric staged; a dream and not a drama." But he described *On Baile's Strand* as one of those experiments "which tend to lilliputianise our legends," and thought Cuchullain was transformed "into a trivial, peckish, and wavering old man."

Passing on to lyric poetry he found the prospect brighter; he praised Yeats, the most powerful influence from Ireland abroad, A.E. the most powerful influence at home, and Lionel Johnson; the rest of his space was devoted to Seamus O'Sullivan's *The Twilight People.* "Metrical music rather than words is his vehicle; a music as of twilight moods audible; a twilight which makes more beautiful the cold divine stars"—the somewhat inflated critique is the better evaluated when we realize that he was puffing a friend.

Abraham Colles, an illustrious nineteenth-century Irish surgeon, advised his students to be single-minded: "If you are clever in anything else but your profession do not let the world know it." Perhaps this conservative tradition made Gogarty adopt the pseudonym "Oliver Gay" for his articles in *The Shanachie* and forced him to realize that soon he must choose, if not exactly between God and Mammon (or should they be reversed?), at any rate between the life of a doctor and the less restricting existence of a writer.

The most important events of 1906-7 for Gogarty were his marriage to Martha Duane of Moyard, Connemara, in August 1906; the conferring of his medical degree in June 1907; and the birth of his first child on July 23. And now Dr. Gogarty had to earn a living. But to that end there was to be a period of post-graduate study in Vienna, for influenced by Mr. (later Sir Robert) Woods he had decided to specialize in ear-nose-and-throat surgery.

In Vienna he rented an apartment once occupied by Krafft-Ebing, worked at the famous Allgemeines Krankenhaus, and adopted the Café Klinik as his postal address. He wrote to James Joyce, pointing out the opportunity that existed for a language teacher among the English-speaking doctors. He wondered if Joyce could find a printer for him and steer "some lighter verse" through the press. He proposed that Joyce should join him on a trip to Athens (Gogarty paying the expenses) and asked him to look out for berths on one of the vessels plying for currants and wine into the gulf of Corinth. But this plan came to nothing; instead Gogarty returned to Dublin in 1908 and put up his shingle.

Joseph Holloway wrote in his diary on May 9, 1908: "Oliver Gogarty has passed his medical exams and is showing great promise as a throat specialist. He has taken Deane's house in Ely Place and sports a motor." A showy motor car, later to be replaced by a butter-colored Rolls-Royce, was the only way a doctor could advertise legitimately; and by purchasing 15 Ely Place from an architect, Gogarty ensured that his house would be comfortable, and fortuitously secured influential neighbors, Sir Thornley Stoker, a leading general surgeon, a source of patients, and George Moore, an easy target for his wit.

Follwing a well-established Dublin tradition of making a butt of Moore, he scored by broadcasting Tyrrell's gibe that the unlettered author of the projected *Ave atque Vale* thought *atque* was a Roman centurion, but Moore emerged creditably from the story of an encounter with Thomas Cook in the Holy Land: the great travel agent's generous offer of a guide to take him to the site of the Holy Sepulchre was turned down by the novelist, who expressed a preference to see the place where the woman was taken in adultery.

2

A Senator Am I !

Myrth is one of the chiefest thynges in physicke. The old adage goes a long way to explain Gogarty's rapid success in practice; what he lacked in experience he compensated for in personality. His physical appearance has been described by Ulick O'Connor in his biography:

> ... he is of average height, five feet nine but appears taller because of his athletic figure. There is a slight effect of broadness about the face, but this is an illusion, as a sculptor's calipers have shown that it is a long narrow head of the northern type. The eyes are striking, vivid blue, so deep in color that his daughter actually remembers there being a shade of violet at times. His hair is brown, but sometimes streaked with gold from the bleaching of the sun, and inclined to stand upright when brushed sideways. There is a fine sweep to the forehead, broad without being over-intellectual; his features are regular, but the nose is slightly large, a characteristic of the Irish face.

Add to his winning manner the good luck he equated with character and his career was assured. At the

Northeastern Junior College
LEARNING RESOURCE CENTER
STERLING, COLORADO 80751 40244

propitious moment Robert Woods resigned from the Richmond Hospital leaving the post of ENT (Ear-Nose-Throat) Surgeon vacant. Gogarty's appointment gave him the experience he needed but provided few private patients. Once more his good angel whispered . . . there was a vacancy at the Meath Hospital . . . if he applied, strings would be pulled. And meanwhile he had taken the much-coveted FRCSI which put the seal on his status as a consultant.

For a time at least he showed an interest in research. His paper to the British Medical Association at its meeting in Aberdeen in July 1914, based on three hundred cases of latent empyema of the nasal sinuses, contained a plea with which any modern ENT surgeon would agree, that no examination of the nose can be considered complete without washing out the antrum of Highmore. He made a vigorous protest against operative injury of the inferior turbinate body which leads to loss of what he called the "air-taste" in the nose. But in the subsequent discussion his recommendation of the use of strong solutions of cocaine suggests that, like many doctors at the time, he was unaware of the dangers of addiction.

His flirtation with medical research never rivaled his lifelong devotion to the Muse. ENT surgery leaves its exponents freer than doctors in other clinical departments and Gogarty found time to spend with old friends and to make new ones. A mercurial conversationalist, his talk ranged from local politics to the Greek classics with the occasional dirty story for good measure. Padraic Colum remembered Gogarty declaiming English, Latin, Greek and lowland Scots poetry throughout an afternoon's walk in the Dublin hills and how "he could take hold of, say, a strophe of Pindar's, recite it, bring before you the whole performance of what would have been the performance of one of the great odes."

And when instead of walking he drove, his passengers were alarmed by the way he took his hands off the steering wheel to emphasize a point, and entranced by his astonishing ability to make the appropriate remark, however ribald. Sweeping past a wedding party with a rural bride, he commented sardonically: "The desire of the cow for the bull, of the mare for the stallion/ The ache of the maid-of-all-work for the private of any battalion."

The drinking habits of early manhood persisted into his thirties. With some of his more dissolute companions he would drink into the small hours. But he rose early, went for a swim, drank a pint of buttermilk and was as ready to face the day as the most sober of his colleagues. He cut out whiskey when he was forty, and later in life his regular tipple in the pubs he frequented was mineral water.

His activity was such that someone said that Gogarty would be happy anywhere except in prison; everywhere else he would be sure to find something to interest him. Archery was a fresh sport to master, and later he was drawn to aviation, probably the first Irish doctor to have a pilot's license.

The Gogartys had three children, Oliver, Dermot and Brenda. Family holidays were spent in Moyard with his hospitable sister-in-law until the purchase of a country property, a sign of increasing affluence, crowned Gogarty's professional success. Set against the background of the Twelve Bens, the *Beana Beola*, the Renvyle Peninsula has a heroic beauty. Approaching it from Moyard and Letterfrack, the road winds and undulates through spartan villages. To either side gray rocks, lake water, brown moorland shot with innumerable greens, and occasional fertile patches where cattle graze and men still bend to the hay with scythes. The road crests a hill beyond the village of Tully and slopes towards the sea: soon the chimneys and roofs of Renvyle House are visible. Originally the home of the Blakes, this mansion was purchased by Gogarty in 1917 and became a literary gathering-place almost as famous as Lady Gregory's Coole Park.

Standing at the front door of Renvyle House, one sees Granuaile's Castle near the tip of the peninsula; to the south Tully Mountain shuts off Letterfrack Bay; to the north the small off-shore islands and farther out Inish Turk and Clare Island—between them far off on the horizon is Achill; to the east and less remote the great bulk of Muilrea, the largest mountain in Connacht and showing above its lower ridge "the Reek," the legendary Croagh Patrick, landmarks which found their way into Gogarty's books.

A lady, who had been a guest in Renvyle House and knew Gogarty well, has said she thought he was a saint *manqué*. If an awareness, of a high order, of the beauty of nature can be equated with holiness and the ability to glorify God's creations in exquisite verse substituted for prayer, there may be a good deal in what she said, but that aspect of his personality has been overshadowed by his reputation as a wit. His humor sometimes depended on a play of words. When introduced to a man named

Story he said, "Welcome to our rough island, Story," and when Mahaffy asked, "Are you rising on a point of order?" he said, "No, on the spur of the moment." But it was often mordant. "Ashe is a fine fellow," he remarked of a colleague, "but he's inclined to think he's the whole cigar." Seeing Lennox Robinson, tall wraith-like and dissipated, he said, "Poached eyes on ghost."

Friends were sacrificed as readily as acquaintances. "Moore isn't a man's man; he's happiest in the company of women of his own sort." "Drink to me with thine only eye," he said to a friend with a glass eye. And in time even Yeats was pilloried. The great poet explained his need for the so-called Steinach rejuvenating operation to a tendency to drop off after lunch, but with caustic realism Gogarty said behind his back, "He has reached the age when he can't take 'Yes' for an answer."

These undiscriminating sallies reflect a hard edge of Gogarty's personality, but however amusing at the time of utterance, finally they served him ill. He was much more than a licensed jester and the crust of wit concealed a compassionate interior. His malicious wit was not in evidence when he delivered an address entitled "The Need of Medical Inspection of School Children in Ireland" to inaugurate the Winter Session of the Meath Hospital in 1911, for the occasion was formal and serious. He may, to be sure, have had a twinkle in his eye when he declared that world conditions were such that "Soon there will be no one healthy," but in his mind's eye was the somber vision of the adenoidal, pigeon-chested, dispirited children who thronged the ENT dispensaries in his hospitals and the mothers who asked him to write notes exempting their offspring from school attendance. He knew that many of the kids came breakfastless to school and few of them had more than a few slices of bread to sustain them through the long school hours. "Feed the school children. The school children must be fed."

That they should be medically inspected, too, was Gogarty's indisputable contention, so that defects could be remedied and those with communicable diseases separated from the healthy. His peroration contains graceful allusions to Greek drama and to Shelley's "We look before and after," but more important for our understanding of Gogarty is its informed and constructive compassion.

> The Greeks, than whom it is our habit to consider ourselves much more humane, had a custom which they later abolished, of exposing weak and undesirable infants. We gained one advantage from this custom—the Sophoclean trilogy.
>
> But can it be said that, after the lapse of years, in this country Christianity has revealed nothing better than a modern method of deserting or neglecting the growing child just as it becomes doubly dependent on us (because of the additional food required for its mind), just as the promised land of life is being revealed to it, and while it is looking only before, and its thoughts are all hopes? From this there is nothing to be gained. Besides, it is much inferior to the ancient method, and a blind and stupid one which neither reasons nor discriminates, but exposes fit and unfit together.

Many of his colleagues had said as much but Gogarty was not content to bury his protest in the pages of a scientific journal. And when his first play *Blight* was staged in the Abbey Theatre in 1917 his motif was the insanitary populous tenements of the Dublin slums, gaunt decayed mansions each housing a score of large families, blighting the lives of its inhabitants, seedbeds of vice and disease. His characters are recognizable types, and as Sean O'Casey was a member of his audience it is not unlikely that drunken Stan Tully lent something to the creation of Joxer Daly and Fluther Good, equally shifty, less comic but more calculating, more authentic.

Tully, the "hero" of *Blight*, is a malingerer who takes advantage of an industrial accident and is compensated by some hundred pounds. His celebratory words are well received. "There was a head on that speech like a pint of stale stout," said the Cabman. A laborer found it "One of them fine reassuring speeches that kept its meaning to itself." And Mrs. Larrissey was overcome: "Wouldn't it put a bull's heart in ye to hear him? The spits of him itself was like a shower iv rain."

Outsmarting his slum landlord, Tully purchases two tenements for a pittance. He is elected to the City Council and to the board of the local hospital which has a legacy to spend—a substantial amount of which will find its way into Tully's pocket, for his tenements stand in the way of the hospital extension scheme.

Gogarty used his knowledge of the sanctimonious do-gooders who serve on hospital boards to create the members of the board of the Townsend Thanatorium, two of which, Norris Galbraith and Tisdall-Townsley, also resemble in some degree George Moore and Sir Thornley Stoker. Mr. Tumulty voices Gogarty's own thoughts about the futility of private charity in the management of public health and knew that prevention is better than cure. "The less you spend on prevention the more you will pay for cure. Until the citizens realize that their children should be brought up in the most beautiful and favourable surroundings the city can afford, and not in the most squalid, until this floundering Moloch of a Government realize that they must spend more money on education than on police, this city will continue to be the breeding-ground of disease, vice, hypocrisy and discontent."

Medical Dick and Medical Davy (also featured in one of Gogarty's bawdiest poems) provide comic relief. Lily Foley with her streetwalker's cynicism—"The wages of sin is a month in the Lock"—outfaces the cold morality of Miss Maxwell-Knox, a district visitor, but as she herself predicted, she is sent to the Lock Hospital with syphilis.

The theme of *A Serious Thing*, Gogarty's one-act play which was staged at the Abbey Theatre on August 19, 1919, during the Black-and-Tan repression, was ostensibly the threat to Roman rule posed by the early Christians in Galilee but its deeper reference was the conflict against British rule in Ireland. Gogarty poked fun at army regulations; his Centurion's "Lookey-here now" was a favorite phrase of Talbot Clifton, a wealthy Englishman who was the author's neighbor in Connemara. It gave him sardonic amusement to see British officers in his audience laughing at the words of the Second Roman: "I'm thinking it's an extraordinary thing that every country we occupy seems to be inhabited exclusively by rebels."

His third play, *The Enchanted Trousers*, was an

amusing one-act satire on bureaucracy and jobbery in rural Ireland. Humphrey Heavey, a hack actor, is persuaded by his brother Andy, a Clare-Galway school-teacher, that all he needs to do to be appointed to a well-paid sinecure is to play the part and wear the costume of an Englishman. The clothes—a Norfolk jacket and knickerbockers—are borrowed by Mrs. Heavey from the local sergeant who had been promoted when he wore them for the King's visit. Mrs. Heavey holds up the trousers for inspection and Andy exclaims, "There you are, Humphrey, when you enter that you enter England." When Humphrey is dressed and stands with a monocle in his eye he looks for all the world a Sassenach, so much so that his brother remarks how he resembles "the auld fellow that blew the tail off the red setter at the Shoot at Moore Hall."

The officials are taken in, Humphrey gets the job with £2,000 a year but behaves hypocritically when it comes to helping his family. This slight piece was staged in the Abbey Theatre on November 25, 1919. It was Gogarty's last play to be staged, but within a few years he himself had a part to play on the larger stage of the Irish Free State Senate where he almost succeeded in getting the Phoenix included in the Wild Bird's Protection Act.

Gogarty had been a member of Sinn Fein since its inception and a close friend of its founder Arthur Griffith, who based his separatist movement on passive resistance. Owing to the tragic events of Irish history, Griffith became the first President of the Irish Free State at a time when the treaty debate culminated in civil war. Eamon de Valera, the leader of the republican party, was henceforth anathema to Gogarty.

Very soon Griffith's health broke down. He was admitted to a nursing home under Gogarty's care and at first improved. But then a brain hemorrhage proved fatal; Gogarty was called but Griffith was already dead. "My poor, poor Arthur," he said, and walking to the window he wept.

President Cosgrave, Griffith's successor, nominated Gogarty as a member of the newly created Irish Free State Senate, an honor which had unexpected repercussions. On a bitter January night in 1923 he was taken from his home at gun-point by political enemies and brought to a house at Islandbridge on the Liffey. "Shall I tip the driver?" he asked his captors, to their annoyance. Subsequently, under the pretext of a call of nature, he eluded the guard, escaped into the darkness and dove into the river. His swim to safety and dripping arrival at the police station was celebrated in a popular ballad of the day that ended as follows:

> Cried Oliver St. John Gogarty, "A Senator am I!
> The rebels I've tricked, the river I've swum, and sorra
>   the word's a lie.'
> As they clad and fed the hero bold, said the sergeant
>   with a wink:
> 'Faith, thin, Oliver St. John Gogarty, ye've too much
>   bounce to sink.'

But the republicans had their revenge. Renvyle House, containing many irreplaceable books and paintings, was burned down. From then on Gogarty had to carry a revolver and have a bodyguard.

As such circumstances disrupted his practice, he took

consulting rooms in London. When his wife seemed unprepared for the domestic upheaval entailed in accompanying him, Lady Dunsany confided in a friend, "She has married a charming flibbertigibbet and a sacrifice is required if she is to keep him [Amory, *Lord Dunsany*, London, 1972]."

He returned every week when the Senate was in session and joined in its debates. On November 28, 1923, he moved the resolution that the Senate congratulate Senator W. B. Yeats on winning the Nobel Prize. "To my mind, since the Treaty, the award of the Nobel Prize to him is the most significant thing that has befallen this country."

His comments often enlivened the debates. Speaking against an amendment to raise the retirement age of judges to seventy-five, he said: "It is not to be suggested that all the senility of the country is to be monopolized by the Bar. It is almost anti-Scriptural to carry on after seventy years of age. I heard a case of an excellent Judge in India who frequently condemned the advocate to death and sometimes addressed the criminal on equal terms." But the author of *Blight* should have known better than to support the regrettable Old Age Pensions Bill which proposed a reduction of the pension by a shilling a week. He applauded the Treasury's attempt "to make us live within our income . . . I am in support of any attempt at retrenchment and I shall support the Bill."

He resumed practice in Dublin in 1924 and held a *salon* on Fridays in Ely Place where the notables included Yeats, A.E., James Stephens, Lennox Robinson, John McCormack, Walter Starkie. Gogarty told stories and the conversation was varied and brilliant; sometimes those who had been on lecture tours in America made fun of their patrons, and on one occasion evoked an outburst of annoyance from John McCormack, who thought the jokes in bad taste. According to Ninette de Valois (*Come Dance With Me*, London 1957), the ensuing silence was broken by Gogarty, who recalled an old dear of his acquaintance who put an end to such moments of embarrassment by putting the question whether it would be preferable to be eaten by a crocodile or an alligator.

Gogarty was not a conversational monopolist; he never ignored a shy person but would draw him out, praise the least thing he said and make a lot of it. Basically he was good-natured, kind and open-hearted. These qualities were to the fore in his home, and the style of the Friday evenings in which his wife played an important part can be gauged from Lady Leslie's gracious tribute.

Glaslough, Co. Monaghan, Dec. 8th.

My Dear Mrs. Gogarty,
  I must send you one line to tell you how very much I enjoyed Friday evening at your house—you are a perfect hostess, and I look on yours, as one of the few remaining 'Salons' in the old meaning of the word. When I came to look for you at the gallery, you had left—so I had no chance of telling you all this!

Yours affectionately,
Leonie Leslie

By the mid-twenties, Gogarty's friendships in Ireland and England reached into all levels of society. He was nevertheless quite as willing as ever to make a joke at his own expense. When he accompanied a pilgrimage to Rome led by President Cosgrave and Dr. Fogarty, Bishop of Killaloe, his card home read: "Yesterday His Holiness the Pope received the Most Reverend Dr. Fogarty and the most irreverent Dr. Gogarty."

3

Medicus Poetae

Poetry is the quintessential verbal expression of the human soul. That look that thrills one's being—that cry—that apprehension of the world's weeping and delight are its legitimate objects; the recognition of courage and poltroonery, the praise of honor, the pricking of absurdity are among its purposes; laughter and beauty—life's saving graces—are its most potent sources.

That this secretion of the emotions, an elixir of the human spirit, should run to rhyme and cadences is at once an enhancement and a disaster, for the analysis of such accidentals holds an irresistible attraction affecting the academic mind like an itch, and there is a related compulsion to catalogue and classify. There is, too a tendency to create hierarchies related latterly to obscurity, the use of symbols and experimentation with form. The situation has a parallel in the medical profession where the research worker attracts greater credit than the clinician, though the latter is actually the fundamental figure. And since clarity is a virtue of Gogarty's verses it may be necessary to remind the obfuscated modern reader that in the House of the Muses, as in Paradise, there are many mansions. That in which the poet in question resided placed a high value on rhyme and rhythm.

> By Rhythm the gods are bound
> The fates in the skein are noosed
> The soul is kin to sound
> And first by sound was loosed.

As a man of action Gogarty was a practitioner of poetry rather than a theorist, and just as in his surgical practice his preoccupation with research was short-lived, the task of the moment a sufficient problem and one to be rapidly completed, so in the practice of poetry the revisals and emendations of more patient craftsmen were uncongenial to his temperament. For him, as Professor Carens has pointed out, poetry was a social act. It need not, of course, be an exclusive occupation—life is too many-sided for that. But in the company of men of like minds it was what mattered most to him. Poetry was a major topic of his correspondence with Joyce and Bell, and apart from such well-known figures as AE, Yeats, and Seumas O'Sullivan, the Bailey coterie George Redding, George Bonass, Tom Kettle, Joseph Boyd Barrett regarded it as an indispensable topic of conversation. When James Stephens joined them he heard for the first time, as he recalled later, "Poetry spoken of with the assured carelessness with which a carpenter talks of his planks and of the chairs and tables and oddments he will make of them."

By his early twenties Oliver Gogarty was already a

competent poet and well-read in poetry, taking as his models the Greek and Latin classics and the English Elizabethans. James Stephens has singled him out as Ireland's only classical poet; F. R. Higgins wrote in a personal letter: "Poetry has many tablelands; yours are peaks scarred with gold—rhythm's mountain ranges illuminated by fastidious craft." Austin Clarke, a dissident voice, has said that he "took every care to avoid the difficult, scarcely-known ways of Irish tradition," and faulted him, perhaps unfairly, for ignorance of Gaelic literature, which makes one feel that Clarke was really complaining because Gogarty's Muse did not link arms with his own. But Gogarty, despite his classical leanings, is very much a national poet though in no narrow sense; and more than any other, he has succeeded in marrying the ancient Mediterranean myths with those of ancient Ireland; his eclecticism reestablishes old links between Irish and European cultures.

Scattered through his prose and verse and in his private letters are informative passages on his views of the functions of poetry and poets. "Verse, if it is to be any good should be as easily called to mind as a wild cherry tree in Spring. It needs no recording." And in a letter to John Drinkwater: "Your poems arrived and I am reading them now and then, when the chance comes, aloud. I think that is the only way poetry should be treated: otherwise it is scriptive and unworthy of the sweet air."

Apart from its utility as a vehicle for delight, poetry has recorded imperishable echoes of "the Long Ago"; the Muse defies Time

Who cuts with his scythe
All things but hers;
All but the blithe
Hexameters.

Through the ages the poet has had his role in peace and
in war:

The bard is of the heights
He sees when all is blind
The heart of passion lights
The prophesying mind.
The sea heaves up, the land
With ruinous guns is locked
What in the dark is scanned,
What in the future locked?
What have the fates to offer
How goes it Gagenhofer?

["Wie geht es Gagenhofer," unpublished poem in
Gogarty's handwriting, written on the blank leaves of
Seumas O'Sullivan's *Requiem* (No. 48), Dublin, 1917, in
the British Museum.]
    Gogarty tells us, too, of his own predilection for "the
lighter lyric line" and he has catalogued the ingredients
of his poetry:

The transient light on the tower,
    The moat in its wintry gold,
Sunlight, and a passing shower,
    The gleam of your garments' fold
That baffles the eye as you pass,
Formless and lovely things
    Like speech that breaks in a laugh . . .

Not for him the epic or long narrative; he was nurtured on the *Greek Anthology* and many of his verses would sit easily in that collection, for example "To the Moon":

> O Born before our birth began!
> Through all your blanched and listening vales,
> Far from the echoing shores of man,
> Aloof, may sing—what nightingales!

But he also celebrated his friends—A.E., "We live too near the eagle and the nest/To know the pinions wide supremacy;" James Stephens, "Where are you, Spirit, who could pass into our hearts and all/Hearts of little children, hearts of trees and hills, and elves?"; Lorcan Galeran, "For whom all Life is but a Feast/And all the world a future Guest!"—and expresses his own well-being,

> I have been full of mirth;
> I have been full of wine;
> And I have trod the earth
> As if it all were mine

and his abiding sense of beauty of the Irish countryside:

> I close my eyes to hold a better sight,
> And all my mind is opened on a scene
> Of oaks with leaves of amber in the green,
> A mist of blue beneath them: to the right
> A long cape fades beyond the azurite
> Of one calm bay to which the pastures lean.
> The rounded fields are warm, and in between
> The yellow gorse is glaring stiff and bright.

It matters little what distraction drives,
Clouds through my mind and breaks the outer day.
For all I know that distant water strives,
Against the land. I have it all my way;
Through budding oaks a steadfast sun survives:
Peace on the fading cape, the waveless bay.

Gogarty had the gift of taking apparently ordinary and everyday things and clothing them with wonderment, making them subjects fit for poetry. "No one sang thee, little fielding . . ." he apostrophized a mushroom. "I first hymned thee here on earth." And then a remarkable simile:

Of all growing things the oddest
    Only of a sudden seen
Unexpected and immodest
    As above a stocking, skin!

A waddling goose, transformed in his imagination, forsakes the shelter of a white-washed gable, regains primordial energy and emulates her high-flying cousins:

There's blue beyond the peak
Of Patrick's frozen Reek.
Oh take on breast and beak
    The night's dark onset.
Washed in the mauve twilight
O'er some far Western bight,
Where islands rest in Light
    Long after sunset!

The delusion that the personal loveliness of today can be preserved for the future by verse is a conceit many poets have indulged, including Ronsard, *"Quand vous*

serez bien vieille, au soir, á la chandelle," and Yeats—
". . . take down this book/And slowly read, and dream
of the soft look/Your eyes had once . . ." But knowing
that to recall it increases the poignancy of lost beauty,
Gogarty ends his poem harshly:

> When your looking-glass no longer
> Throws enchantment back again,
> That enchantment which was stronger
> Than you guessed on lives of men,
> Take my book to find reflected,
> Safe from ravage of the years,
> All the pride by time rejected:
> Only then break into tears.

If juvenilia existed, nothing is known of them. The
earliest lyrics were sent to Bell; to Joyce he sent bawdy
verses, and to a poem featuring Medical Dick and
Medical Davy he appended notes which reflect his lack
of admiration for academic criticism.

> Notice the almost severe manner in which the legend opens.
> No details diminish the naked and sublime conception of
> the protagonists. . . Stanza II line iii carefully observes the
> deprecatory past subjunctive tense in the 'I'd swap' for 'I
> would swap.' It is in order to avoid emphasis. . . The name
> too is symbolic. Did not the stones of David overcome the
> ponderous Goliath?

The prize-winning "poems" awarded the Vice-Chancel-
lor's Prize were exercises in versifying rather than
poetry. The early love lyrics in *Dana* ("To Stella" and
"Winnifred," 1904, "Molly," 1905) fall well short of
perfection but the "Two Songs" published in *The*

Venture (1905) are of a different quality. The vowel-music of the black "a's" in the first of these is singularly effective.

> My love is dark, but she is fair;
>   As dark as damask roses are,
> As dark as woodland lake-water,
>   Which mirrors every star.

Many of Gogarty's early verses were love poems, the poems of love lost and won; the wanton musings of young men in days before the mini-skirt spoiled speculation. A lost love evoked some perfect lines:

> Begone, sweet Ghost, O get you gone!
> Or haunt me with your body on:
> And in that lovely terror stay
> To haunt me happy night and day.
> For when you come I miss it most,
> Begone, sweet Ghost!

and predatory thoughts prompted "To the Maids not to Walk in the Wind":

> But when your clothes reveal your thighs,
>   And surge around your knees,
> Until from foam you seem to rise
>   Like Venus from the seas. . . .
>
> Though ye are fair, it is not fair!
>   Unless ye will be kind,
> Till I am dead *and changed to air*,
>   O walk not in the wind!

Predictably his output was reduced by medical

commitments; furthermore he had to remember that a poet's mantle does not fit snugly over the white coat of a doctor. Fifteen of his poems were included in the anonymous collection edited by Susan Mitchell, *Secret Springs of Dublin Song*. These were mainly humorous verses such as "A Lament for George Moore":

> Lonely, O Moore, your old friends are;
>   We miss you; and, forgive the banter,
> We miss the generous cigar,
>   The coy decanter

—and the parody on Yeats's "The Old Men Admiring Themselves in the Water":

> I heard the old, old man say:
>   'Mineral Waters,
> The doctor ordered me lithia.'
> His face was like the face one sees
> In Galway county families
>   By the halters
> Of flapper meetings led astray,
> Where tide is low and bookies' pay
>   Mostly falters.
> I heard the old, old man say:
> 'What do you think will win today
>   By the waters?'

But there is a hint, too, of the social awareness that later led to *Blight* in his "Ballad of Dublin" for the magical twilights conceal

> Pestilence, sorrow and poverty's lair,
> Pride's in a grandeur overthrown,
> Bawdy and faithful, squalid and fair—
> And winding Liffey in Dublin Town.

Only twenty-five copies of Gogarty's first book, *Hyperthuleana*, were printed for private circulation. *The Ship and Other Poems* is an insubstantial booklet containing five poems, and Gogarty's first real bow before the public as an accomplished poet did not take place until 1923 when *An Offering of Swans*—awarded the Tailteann gold medal for poetry in 1924—was published by the Cuala Press. Even this was a limited edition, but in March 1924 he mentioned a forthcoming London edition in a letter to Seymour Leslie: "Spottiswoode is about to publish a book of mine with 30 additional pieces. They have up to now published only Bibles. I am such a suitable successor to that inconsequent volume that I look naturally forward to all the parsons and village libraries stocking me."

He was in his fiftieth year when *Wild Apples*, his next collection, was published in a small edition of fifty copies—"Here are wild apples/Here's a tart crop!" A second and larger edition (250 copies) differing somewhat in content came out in 1932. The tartness was not much in evidence, his lines still largely inspired by the Muse he had addressed in *Hyperthuleana:*

Flushed is your bonnie face,
Cambered your belly
Muse, like the straying Grace
In Botticelli.
Wild with the fruit and blooms'
Mystical birth
Which the dark wood illumes,
Drunken with mirth.

An instinctive aristocrat, Gogarty could admire the invading Normans who

> Brought rigid law, the long spear and the horsemen
> Riding in steel; and the rhymed, romantic, high line;
> Built those square keeps on the forts of the Norsemen,
>   Still on our sky-line.

His partiality was for the company of "Tall unpopular men/ Slim proud women. . ." but he knew that for others there were different visions:

> Yet who shall say our housemaid's evenings out
> Hold less of the romantic, though she hear
> No stricken steeds nor armed Ajax shout,
> Nor see the tranced forest dimly lit?
> The cabmen and the soldiers still are here—
> She's twenty-one, and that makes up for it!

And at La Trappe, confronted with the incongruity of naked legs, his own fancies did not balk at the prospect of demotic impropriety:

> And then I prayed a little space
> 'O, Thou Lord God, what is this thing
> Besets me in Thine Holy Place?
> Why must Thy washerwoman fling
> Her petticoats before my face
> And set me wild with wantoning?
> O, cool me with Thine Holy Water
> That I may think not on her daughter!'

Others to Adorn (1938) is a fairly comprehensive selection from earlier books, with some additions. *The Collected Poems* (1950) seems to have been compiled on haphazard principles but presumably does indicate which of his verses Gogarty considered worth preserving. Nevertheless, some inferior poems are included while others, possibly more interesting, are dropped. The Ode to mark the revival of the Tailteann Games has

the faults of such official effusions so often rhetorical
rather than poetical. The "Bi-Centenary Ode," equally
defective, is only mentioned here because few present-
day readers will have seen it. Written for the bicenten-
ary of the School of Physic, it was read in the Queen's
Theatre by Professor Tyrrell as a prologue to a special
performance of *She Stoops to Conquer*. Its best lines are
those depicting the city in the eighteenth century when

> The rose-red Georgian houses seem
> To catch a glory and to gleam
>   As when their lights of old
> Shone out, with many a taper's blaze,
> On Dublin of the bounteous days.
>   Built by the liberal and the bold
> In spacious street and square.
>   What memories are theirs to hold
> Of gallant and of fair;
> Each room a house, each house a town
>   Each hall a thoroughfare!

and his hint of the blood-letting doctors of an earlier
period:

> Thus lived they, fighting, gaming, supping
> And never people needed cupping
>   So much—And O they were not spared!
> Their lives were full, their deeds were doughty
> And God who made all good things gouty
>   Did not withhold their lives' reward,
> Except from those who, once too sporty,
> With dropped wrist died from lead at forty,
>   But died in times that did not reach
> To atheroma or retention
> Which Metchnikoff and Osler mention
>   Who do not practice what they preach.

This evocation of pathology serves to underline the

unobtrusive fact that Gogarty's days were spent caring
for the ailing. A clinician recalls more readily than
others jarring realities that mar the spring:

> New dogs at every corner range,
> New Limericks fill the Stock Exchange,
> The ducks now splash in Stephen's Green,
> Where cripples on the benches lean,
> And merrily the children race
> Round noseless men with half a face—

and in "Medicus Poetae" he emphasizes that his path
does not run through sylvan ways:

> But I by bed and in the lazer-house
> Where misery the Feast of Life derides
> And Death confuses Autumn with the Spring,
> Can sometimes, though I see not Beauty's brows,
> Catch the uncertain syllable that bids
> The blackbird leap from his dark hedge and sing.

Gogarty has been compared to Herrick, but he is an
Irish Herrick. His ladies and landscapes are Irish though
linked to Greece in his mind, which joined the Mediterranean littoral to Lettergesh in Connemara where he
drove with Augustus John on a corniche road

> . . . .above the shine
> Of the green and grapy sea,
> Whose translucent greenery
> Broke on crescent sands remote,
> Goldener than Helen's throat.

The orderliness of the English countryside, which
Gogarty wearied of in *Going Native*, has no counterpart
in untidy, neglectful Ireland:

A bank of tangled briars
Sloped gently to the south,
Its leaves recalled her mouth
With their soft hidden fires.
"Her lips are bright as cherries
And sweet as wild strawberries,"
I said. Where leaves were spangled
The wild rose grew more tangled
With barbed and bending wires.

Feminine enchantment and allure are vivid in verses commemorating the nubile lassies of *Dana*, riper beauty,

Like a tall Saint who clasps upon her breast
A Pindar hidden by a palimpsest

and the sweetness of childhood. His daughter, Brenda, inspired "Golden Stockings" and a neighbor's child evoked the following lines:

You in your apple-tree
In your sun bonnet
(Ribbands upon it),
Dimples that laugh at me!
Thus you came into view
Over our hedge,
Blithe as the light on you
At the lips' edge!

Surprisingly for a poet so joyous whose pages frequently reflect the resurgence of the year:

soon they'll tingle in the blue
And all their amber joy renew;
And transubstantiate to wood
The Spring's impalpable new blood

—a constant theme is mutability,

Beauty yet to come, Beauty gone before;

The uninterruptable implacable procession and death:

> When April with its secret green
> Is felt no more but only seen;
> And Summer with its dusky meadows
> Is no more than a play of shadows;
> And Autumn's garish oriflamme
> Fades like a flickering skiagram;
> And all one's friends are gone, or seem
> Shadows of dream beyond a dream. . . .

This unexpected apprehension of morbidity may be a token of the melancholy disclosed to Bell or the outcome of the professional confrontation expressed in "All the Pictures":

> I told him he would soon be dead.
> 'I have seen all the pictures,' said
> My patient. 'And I do not care.'
> What could a doctor do but stare
> In admiration. . . .

In days when aural suppuration was rife and its complications lethal, he must have seen many children sicken:

> Death may be very gentle after all:
> He turns his face away from arrogant knights
> Who fling themselves against him in their flights;
> But to the lovliest he loves to call.
> And he has with him those whose ways were mild
> And beautiful; and many a little child.

If the academic love of labels is to be satisfied, Gogarty will be classified as a "minor" poet and one must say how regrettable it is that unlike international football players, opera stars and couturiers (all of whom would be accepted as "first-class"), poets not ranking as major are qualified with a diminishing adjective. His performance was uneven. He took the easy way out, satisfied too often with a facile rhyme, and to avoid redrafting he would leave an imperfect line. A perusal of the different existing versions of various poems shows that his alterations were minimal. And he is unfortunate that at present a metrical sense is as out-of-date as a Viennese waltz. But presumably that lovely expression of the human spirit will not remain permanently neglected.

He wrote many exquisite lyrics. "The Image-Maker" may be cited as an example of his perfection of this form.

> If but the will be firmly bent
> No stuff resists the mind's intent;
> The adamant abets his skill
> And sternly aids the artist's will,
> To clothe in perdurable pride
> Beauty his transient eye descried.

Yet the characteristic Gogarty is in the mock-heroic. Poems such as "To a Cock" and "Leda and the Swan," which must be read in their entirety, are uniquely his, or such a *jeux d'esprit* as "After Galen," which nobody should miss.

Vivien Mercier (*Poetry* [1958]) sees "Leda and the Swan" as a masterpiece of sustained tone running a razor's edge between irony and farce and asks, "Why do the critics who like to talk about wit, irony and ambiguity never take up this poem, though they love to study Yeats's companion piece? If you think Gogarty's piece was easier to write than the Yeats sonnet just try to produce a similar *tour de force.*"

Certainly Gogarty has been ignored by the critics. Professor A. Norman Jeffares, who took the "ear, nose, and throat specialist with an ear for melody, a nose for the ridiculous, and a throat unashamed of emotional speech and song" as the subject of his Chatterton Lecture, is an exception. "The Ship" reminds Jeffares of Flecker; he places Eliot's "newspapers from vacant lots" in amusing juxtaposition with the Irishman's more optimistic

> By an old lot a cherry tree
> An old wild cherry blooming brightly
> A sight of joy in the unsightly.

He finds the clarity and excitement of Marvell's "green Thought in a green Shade" in Gogarty's "Fresh Fields":

> I gaze and gaze when I behold
> The meadows springing green and gold.
> I gaze until my mind is naught
> But wonderful and wordless thought!
> Till, suddenly, surpassing wit,
> Spontaneous meadows spring in it;
> And I am but a glass between
> Un-walked-in meadows gold and green.

—and remarks that the love poems "have the ease of Horace and the same amount, perhaps, of sincerity."

Jeffares places the poems in three groups: descriptive verses often graced by heroes of Irish history; poems of attitude related to the Irish state of mind; and classico-romantic poetry, the most important achievement.

It weds a tension in its author. It has the direct speech and
economy of classicism, yet it captures romantic awareness
of immediacy of life. Its basis is the realization that "Man is
in love and loves what vanishes." It says this, but does not
add, "What more is there to say?": its romantic vocabu-
lary, sometimes carried easily, sometimes very uneasily
indeed by its classical syntax, served both the poet's objective mind as well as the emotional impulses and instincts of
his human heart.

Jeffares suggests that Gogarty may have himself to
thank for being undervalued; like Goldsmith and unlike
Yeats, who invariably projected himself as a serious
poet, he chose the masks of a joker. He finds that Yeats
and Gogarty offer some interesting parallels. The latter
has indicated that he was receptive to the older man's
constructive suggestions but it seems, too, that
Gogarty's ideas were sometimes developed by Yeats
who placed him among the "swift indifferent men" that
he admired.

In a postscript to a letter asking permission to include
a number of Gogarty's poems in the anthology he was
editing, W. B. Yeats wrote: "I think you are perhaps
the greatest master of the pure lyric now writing in
English. I am asking for a lot, but don't charge me too
much. I can get you a thousand readers for every ten
your publisher can get you." Subsequently Yeats
thanked Gogarty for the required permission which, presumably, the latter was very glad to give, "and for your
nobility in omitting the 'jingle of the guinea'."

Curiously, the inclusion of seventeen of his poems in
the *Oxford Book of Modern Verse* (1936) has often
been cited to Gogarty's discredit. It needs only a swing
of fashion, restoring parity to melody and allowing

bright images to penetrate the gloom, to vindicate the
editor. Meanwhile, can one do other than ascribe a lot
of the ill-feeling caused by Yeats's selection to spite, a
by-product of envy? But in any case, if poetry is written
for anyone except the author it certainly is not prima-
rily intended for other poets and academics; and while
their more stringent opinions seem to rank unduly, what
really matters is the usually unheard voice of the general
reader.

An appreciative Scotsman probably spoke for many
when expressing his feelings in a letter to Gogarty.

> It is a good many years since I first came across a selection
> of your poems in the *Oxford Book of Modern Verse* and
> finding you in the dry and thirsty Wasteland of most of the
> moderns was like coming upon a well of water. It was with
> the greatest eagerness that I ordered a copy of your *Col-
> lected Poems* as soon as I saw them advertised and it is with
> the utmost pride that I now possess one. They seem to me
> to have wit, gaiety, wisdom and courage as well as formal
> beauty and clarity of language—and heart. I have found
> enormous comfort as well as pleasure in them; and not a
> few of them (as for example, *"Per Iter Tenebricosum"*) are
> of that perfection which sends a shiver down the spine, like
> great music, and seem to me as fine as anything I have come
> across in English literature.

Another admirer of his verse, a soldier's wife, wrote to
say that she was taking his *Collected Poems* with her to
Malaya: "I do not know whether you will find the
necessity of taking it to a wooden house in a jungle
clearing in Pahang a tribute to the poems or an insult to
the binding . . . but I promise that it will be valued very
much. They are poems to read and re-read until they are

kept in the heart not locked in a dustproof bookshelf as a collector's edition."

Such untutored testimonies have an important validity but for those fresh from the lecture rooms and for axe-grinding Dubliners unwilling to bestow the accolade on a local the judgment of W. B. Yeats may be reiterated: Yeats in his introduction to the *Oxford Book of Modern Verse* proclaimed Gogarty as "one of the great lyric poets of our age." Why then should lesser men cavil?

4

Sackville Street

The 1930s found Gogarty in his fifties and in his prime. According to a friend, he was "twenty-five years younger than anyone should be at his age at any particular time—in outlook, in physique, in everything about him." The Minister of Defense, Mr. Frank Aiken, referred to him as "a lazy body" and was challenged to a duel to take the form of an athletic contest in the air, on the earth, and in the water, a challenge which, although by much the younger man, the Minister did not accept.

Gogarty was a deft surgeon with good hands and good judgment but his professional reputation may have owed something to legendary inflation. When an anaesthetist who worked with him said, "He's the King of all antrum operators," a junior colleague demurred: "The King? Hardly! Maybe the Old Pretender!" But by this time, in any case, he was losing interest in surgery and tiring of patients, having, as he said, looked down their throats and up their noses long enough. When invited to join the newly formed section of Laryngology, and Otology of the Royal Academy of

Medicine in Ireland he declined, saying he didn't wish to be standardized.

Long before the importance of tourism was generally appreciated Gogarty pointed out its potentiality for helping the national economy. "We have all the shipping companies of the Atlantic knocking at the door, and we have not the sense to open the shop." A deep-water pier should be built at Galway.

> If you take a mercator map (not the medieval flat atlas that is still used for misleading schoolchildren) it will be apparent that the nearest to America of all the bays in Europe is Galway Bay. It is also one of the safest harbours and freest from fogs. (*Daily Express*, July 25, 1930)

The rebuilt Renvyle House was opened as a hotel; henceforth the guests who appealed to Gogarty's gregarious nature would pay for their keep. Mine host's intention was to supplement his income further by his pen. He contributed occasional articles to the *Daily Express*, the *Evening Standard*, and other papers. He spent the first three months of 1933 on a lecture tour in America and between times he was working on a book which brought him fame and notoriety when published in 1937.

In the intervening years his older friends began to step into the shadows. George Moore died in 1933 and his ashes were taken to where Moore Hall stood in ruins in County Mayo, the urn placed on an island in Loch Carra. A sad day, not to be forgotten.

> No! That day on that lake by me will never be forgotten: the oars that dipped in silence and the funerary urn held by Moore's sister in the stern of the heavy boat. We

two were alone and we spoke but little, for it was a sad passage with the ashes of a man we loved between us; but as the ripples broke the lake's surface, they laughed, danced, sparkled, and laughed again, they were like millions of invulnerable and immortal merrimen rejoicing that a spirit, as native and as impish as their own, the spirit of the last squire of Ireland, and unageing artist had mingled with them after a long sojourn on earth in his unparallelable life.

Two years later the news that A.E. was dying so moved Gogarty that with the mixed instincts of a doctor and a friend he hurried to England to offer aid or bid adieu. On the following day he wrote in the *Irish Times:* "The most magnanimous Irishman of our generation is dead ... [he] died with his work finished and the contribution of a great soul complete."

Such griefs are inseparable from life. On a less desolate occasion Gogarty expressed impishness: "As for weeping — I feel more inclined to turn upon the toe." His antic disposition was to the fore at the Irish Academy of Letters dinner to celebrate Lord Dunsany's election when he said, "Since this Academy was formed to keep Dunsany out we ought to dissolve it now that he's admitted."

"Quaintly he came raiking out of Molesworth Street into Kildare Street, an odd figure moidered by memories. . ." Thus from the passing show Gogarty picked out "Endymion," a Dublin character who among other peculiarities of dress wore his cuffs on his ankles to indicate that he was standing on his hands. In the National Library register Endymion signs himself James Boyle Tisdell Burke Stewart Fitzsimons Farrell (a name familiar to readers of *Ulysses*) and Gogarty realized that the harmless lunatic was engaged in presenting a cavalcade of Dublin life backwards for thirty years and decided to emulate him. *As I Was Going Down Sackville Street,* Gogarty's first prose work, winds backwards leisurely from the mid-thirties, meandering just as willfully through the decades as the River Liffey does in its course from Kippure and Poulaphouca to the Strawberry Beds until enmities are forgotten and shadows dissolve in bright recollections of a time before the First World War when a picnic could be the most important thing in life.

The title derives from a ballad composed when Sackville Street (now O'Connell Street) was the principal avenue of the city which is the hero of his book, a hero which he defends from autochthonous despoilers who have replaced its former masters. The latter are admired and chided in turn: Gogarty had a largeness of mind that could admire British civilization at its best but contained sufficient of the national disillusion to remember to fear three things, the hoofs of a horse, the horns of a bull, and the smile of a Saxon.

His intention of writing a book on Oliver Goldsmith and the Johnson circle never materialized but he used the other Oliver's lines to express dismay on finding his country "peopled by surly men nursing an immemorial grievance or inventing one to their peculiar consciences to justify outrage."

> *Ill fares the land to hastening ills a prey*
> *Where louts accumulate and lords decay.*

Sackville Street is an uncompromising book. Few other than Irish readers will appreciate to what degree it must have incensed those who differed politically from its author. Sacred cows and national heroes are treated with a candor astonishing for the thirties, however commonplace today. The "hard political women" and the Irregulars who took the Republican side in the Civil War, according to temperament, should have withered under his scorn or perished from rage on reading his pages.

> I could never countenance this euphuism 'Irregulars.' They were simply the town blackguards misled, or country dupes and discontents whom de Valera aroused when he found that his slimness and duplicity had landed him in a minority.

And not until recently when Conor Cruise-O'Brien spoke out against the National cult of necrophilia has any Irishman so forcefully condemned the unhealthy adulation of political martyrs. "Damn the vampire dead who have left us nothing but a heritage of hatred. . ."

Fearing that the liberated Kathleen Ni Houlihan was becoming a soured harridan, Gogarty expressed his alarm with accustomed vehemence. He viewed the new political leaders with a suspicion that time has justified. What was their idea of a nation likely to be? "Would it give leave to live to all its Nationals? Would its idea of freedom be universal or restricted to a gang?"

> The Bagmen with their little despatch cases are for the moment in insurrection, and it is against Milesians they are revolting. And they are in the ascendancy just now. This explains a great deal. It explains the desire not to be thought 'Irish' in the narrow and narrowing sense which that word has come at present to have. They do not wish to be identified with all that is small, narrow, vindictive, cowardly, and vile. Irishmen, be they de Burgoes or Milesians, are not happy with this 'Freedom' which has only thrown them to the mercy of the tinkers in the land.

Sackville Street, however controversial in the thirties, expressed views which are perfectly acceptable today to anyone untouched by political hagiology.

Reminded of *Hail and Farewell,* Terence de Vere White said it was Moore again, with less malice and less art. But there is enough malice to pepper the pages, and some to spare. Literary "friends" fared hardly better than political enemies. Any dereliction of friendship is forgotten, however, as one marvels over sentences that peg out Edward Martyn like a specimen on a laboratory bench. "But suddenly a fat shout from the plain oaken chair." "His gills cardinalised into crimson."

Sackville Street is thronged with Gogarty's contemporaries under their own names and as thinly disguised fictional characters such as Thwackhurst the graffiti-collector, in reality "Sodomy" Cox, a barrister who earned his sobriquet by expressing sympathy for Oscar Wilde. Senator Fanning was amused to be made the vehicle of Gogarty's own indignation, ex-President Cosgrave took in good part the comment that his piety had embarrassed the Pope, but Harry Sinclair, a Jewish antique dealer, was granted an injunction restraining further publication of the book, which his affidavit described as "a resevoir of filth and the grosser forms of vulgarity," pending a trial for libel.

Sinclair was offended by verses which, he alleged, referred to himself and his twin brother, William Abraham Sinclair:

Two Jews grew in Sackville Street
   And not in Piccadilly.
One was gaitered on the feet,
   The other one was Willie.

And if you took your pick of them,
    whichever one you chose,
You'd like the other more than him,
    So wistful were those Jews.

Another defamatory passage, he claimed, charged the
Sinclairs and their grandfather, Morris Harris, with
immorality.

Now, there was an old usurer who had eyes like a pair of
periwinkles on which somebody had been experimenting
with a pin, and a nose like a shrunken tomato, one side of
which swung independently of the other. The older he grew
the more he pursued the immature, and enticed little girls
into his office. That was bad enough; but he had grandsons,
and these directed the steps of their youth to follow in
grandfather's footsteps, with more zeal than discrimination.

When the libel action was heard in November 1937 a
judgment was given against Gogarty; the plaintiff was
awarded nine hundred pounds damages. *Sackville Street*
had been a costly publication for Gogarty but this did
not curb his outspokenness. One feels that he would
have been at ease in the company of Villon or Ben
Johnson. He upheld the tradition of the literary pubs
that it is better to lose a friend (or a libel action) than a
jest. His comments offended some of his acquaintances
but others, like Frank O'Connor, whom he described as
"a country boy with hair in his nose and hair in his ears
and a briefcase in his hand", were magnanimous, real-
izing as O'Connor tells us in *My Father's Son,* that the
kind heart was a truer measure of the man than the
unbridled tongue. When someone said to Mrs. Yeats that
"at this minute he's sitting somewhere saying scandalous
things" she said, "And don't you know that a man can

do that and still be the most loyal friend you ever had."
She had good reasons for her discernment: years previously Gogarty had tried to set up W. B. Yeats as a prospective professor of English Literature at TCD; in the twenties his influence placed Yeats in the Senate; in the thirties he secured the benefaction which relieved Yeats from financial worries.

His friend Kevin O'Sheil found him charming, "a perpetual boy" and, surprisingly, thought he had a "love of sense of proportion." His political pronouncements lacked that sense; his diatribes against the Fianna Fail government were notorious and it has been said that the jury in the libel case would have awarded nominal damages were it not that a juryman insisted that "even if what he had said about the Jewman didn't matter so much the defendant must be made suffer for all the things he had said about de Valera." Yet, a London newspaper columnist picking a dozen companions for a desert-island stranding chose as follows: Socrates, St. Francis, Leonardo da Vinci, Villon, Rabelais, Shakespeare, Dr. Johnson, Burns, Shaw, Ninon de l'Enclos, Florence Nightingale, Mrs. Beeton, and Olivei St. John Gogarty.

Terence de Vere White recalled meeting Gogarty, who knew him by sight, if not by name — "Hello, Pearson," he sometimes said when he saw the younger man in the street — and being taken into the doctor's study and given a signed copy of a recently published book. Despite his position and achievement Gogarty showed no trace of pomp or conceit.

His amusing and malicious remarks continued to circulate. "If a Queen bee were crossed with a Friesian

bull might not the country flow with milk and honey?"
And of a colleague with a disproportionately large
medical practice: "He dislikes walking in Stephen's
Green because on his approach the ducks always cry
'quack!'" He dismissed the Mona Lisa smile as the ef-
fects of an ill-fitting denture. His amusing retort to a
lady member of the Irish Aero Club was probably taken
in good part. They were discussing planes and she said,
"You should get a Moth." "Oh, no," he said, "I'm
afraid you wouldn't hold a candle to it." His quip about
a critic − "He read the wrong edition" ' − evoked a
question, "Well, what edition should he have read?"
which earned a demolishing reply "The Braille edition!"
And during an acrimonious Senate debate when an
opponent asked" Is it to be a battle of wits?" Gogarty's
riposte was that he would never fight an unarmed man.

His penchant for vituperation evoked like responses
from those of similar temperament and these continue.
A contemporary critic referred to "his Pooh Bah birth-
mark." A reviewer of *Sackville Street* wrote, "It seems
now that he spent a lot of his time as a hanger-on of the
big shots, collecting mud to throw at them." The
Catholic Bulletin designated him among the New
Ascendancy it despised and said that his "Offering to
Swans" (sic) was modeled "on the ugly duckling which
waddled forth in one stanza of the Trinity College Ode,
or even on the goose presented to the Tailteann Com-
mittee." When he went on the American lecture tour in
1933 the same journal placed him with the "carpet-
bagger literati":

One of the best pieces of advertising on the part of Oliver

St. John Gogarty was being featured in a New York daily with John McCormack and Yeats and Joseph Campbell. It is quite possible that Campbell may not know of what discerning Irishmen think of Yeats, Gogarty and Co., but John McCormack's recent sojourn in Ireland gives him no excuse.

Fortunately the controversial issue in his next book, the birthplace of a saint, was unlikely to cause litigation or do more than make scholars raise their eyebrows. In *I Follow Saint Patrick* we are taken by a companionable guide to places hallowed by association with "a Columbus of the Faith to the Gael." He approaches his theme in a roundabout way: "As I stood by the wall of Mycenae under the Lion Gate, I thought of Ard Macha and of Niall of the Nine Hostages"; in Bristol he went to the docks"—that is where the coastwise men are to be found"; in Dublin he consulted a metallurgist who took him to a workshop in Harcourt Street basement and showed him the inutility of bronze swords; he obtained new insights in the verses of Claudian.

Having studied the biographies and personally surveyed the terrains in question he is prepared to back his own conclusion that *Bannavem Taburniae,* Patrick's father's village, was near St. David's in South Wales and puts forward the suggestion that "it was a fleet of Niall of the Nine Hostages which captured Patrick in the year of that King's death at sea. . . ."

The main facts concerning Patrick's apostolate are well known: sold into slavery in Ireland, he was commanded in a dream to escape; eventually he returned to convert the country of his captivity to Christianity. Gogarty pictures no meek saint but a "fiery and zealous man."

His skill in topographical description is exemplified in the account of Patrick at Slane:

> The Hill of Slane is the grandest hill in Meath. As they ascended it by the path which comes off the road to Ardee, about a mile from the river, the great Plain of Hills spread more and more widely behind them. Away to the south-west, in the white evening brightness, the roofs of Tara could be seen breaking the long, level line like a crown. The mighty Hall of Mead Circling, built of old by Cormac, stood loftiest, with its great gables rising thirty-five cubits high. The rounded tops of the entrenched palaces were defined in dark shadows as the sun went down.

His advantage over the conventional historians is his ability to create vignettes. He brings Totus Calvus, the Saint's bald charioteer, before us with striking clarity: "I could see Totus swinging the natty cobs into the plain of Murrisk with the pole rattling as he trotted them in." With an ingenuity born of his knowledge of literature, he links Saint Patrick's Purgatory with Provence through the translations of Marie de France, the Queen of Troubadours.

He followed the Saint to the penitential mountain in Connaught, which at the time of Patrick's fast was called Mount Aigli but is now named for him, and to Caher Island, the most westerly point of his journey. On a clear day Croagh Patrick is a salient on the horizon viewed from the ridge of Renvyle near the old Coast-guard Station a mile from Gogarty's hotel:

> Away to the north, thirty miles away, it stands with its cone lucent and silvern, far-seen, recessed in light like a mountain in Elysium. In the middle distance the great mole of Muilrea looms to the east across the bay which it forms

by extending one long low limb to the west over which the cone appears. Muilrea looms lambent and purple like the substance of a dream.

Caher Island "which lies like a wedge with its raised base oceanwards" is a formidable distance off-shore from Murrisk, Patrick's embarkation point, but more easily reached from Renvyle Point. Thus it appears that Gogarty's interest in Saint Patrick (for he was not an instinctive hagiographer) was determined by the circumstances which attached him to Renvyle.

Connemara provided many images for Gogarty's poetry and could on occasion provide an element of adventure. Early on an April morning in 1938 the *Daisy Star*, outward bound from Westport, struck a rock at low tide and was in danger of foundering. The ship's boy swam five hundred yards to shore and raised the alarm at Renvyle House, Gogarty and his son gave what assistance they could; they took a boat from the lake by the hotel and set out for the damaged vessel where they helped to stanch a hole in the bows. And with accustomed cynicism Gogarty told a reporter "It was an ideal day for a shipwreck. Dawn was breaking. Incidentally, so was the ship."

January 1939 brought the news that W. B. Yeats was dead, and in March Gogarty again featured in a libel case. On this occasion he was the plaintiff, and was awarded a hundred pounds damages against Michael Joseph, Ltd., publishers of Patrick Kavanagh's *The Green Fool*. The offending comment; "I mistook Gogarty's white-robed maid for his wife or his mistress; I expected every poet to have a spare wife," was so mild that people may have wondered if a sore spot had been touched.

From Connemara he wrote to Dr. Patrick MacCartan:

> Before coming down here to finish *Tumbling in the Hay* I sent two periodicals containing reviews on *St. Patrick*. All the reviews were astonishingly favourable and whatever market Ireland presents will be glutted... It should have good sales in the U.S.A. though I find that I get better returns from Europe as well as better advance royalties.

Tumbling in the Hay, which was published in 1939, is buoyant with youthful memories; it is a joyous, exuberant book, free of the animadversions and disillusion of *Sackville Street*, a worthwhile contribution to literature. Narrated by Gideon Ousley, a transparent disguise for Gogarty himself, it introduces a host of splendid characters limned from life but touched up with artistic skill.

Commencing with a cab journey that takes young Ousley from Cecilia Street medical school (so convenient to Mr. Golly's tavern) to deposit him instead in Trinity College, it finishes six years later with another cab drive (in the Smallpox Cab this time) on a night when Doctor Ousley and his newly qualified friends stand at the end of the irresponsible days that have brought them to the threshold of their professional careers.

In more serious moments of the intervening years a teacher in the Richmond Hospital has warned them that for them the future lies

> with the dying and the diseased. The sunny days will not be yours any longer but days in the crowded dispensaries

where you must render service. It is in the darkened pathological department of some institution that you, some of you, will spend your lives in tireless investigation of that microcosmic world which holds more numerous and more dangerous enemies of man than the deep. Your faces will alter. You will lose your youthful smirks; for, in the end, your ceaseless traffic with suffering will reflect itself in grave lines upon your countenance. Your outlook on life will have none of the deception that is the unconscious support of the layman; to you all life will appear in transit, and you will see with clear and undeceived vision the different stages of its devolution and its undivertible path to the grave.

Perhaps this confrontation of youth with the harshness of Nature's decrees explains the levity of the medicals, traditionally the wildest of all students. Ousley's friends, Weary Mac, the Citizen, and Silly Barney are typical of the ilk; the four Halogens ("Dolan, Hegarty, McCluskey and Roowan, never found free in Nature, always combined!") are more studious.

Sooner or later they all had to burn the midnight oil, for an immense body of knowledge has to be assimilated by aspirants to a medical degree. Verse was a convenient aide-memoire for Gogarty/Ousley in anatomy:

"I'm going to swerve,"
Said the lingual nerve.
"Well be sure you avoid,"
Said the pterygoid,
"Myself and the ramus
When passing between us."
"Oh, you'll be bucked,"
Said Wharton's duct,
"When you land in the kip
At the tongue's top tip."

It assisted too in therapeutics: "Hydrarg. perchlor. and Pot. Iod./For those who don't believe in God," and when regulating the diets of fever cases:

> Fluid, farinaceious, fish;
> Then a chicken in a dish;
> Then to mutton, then to beef;
> Then from all rules there is relief!

Gogarty was no ordinary medico. He could walk with kings as represented by Mahaffy, Tyrrell, and Macran (Dons admirable! Dons of Might! to mix not metaphors but poets) nor lose the common touch that made him at home in Golly's and in Nighttown.

His description of his tutor is far more effective than the mindless invective hurled across the generation gap by today's undergraduates:

> His gown flying out behind him, his grey striped trousers gone at the knees from much sitting, my Tutor crossed in front of the Chapel, blear-eyed, rushing into the Past. He was blear-eyed from staring at old papyri on which he doubtless considered me to be a nasty little palimpsest.

His ability to discern the hilarity concealed by an unprepossessing exterior enabled him to invest a dubious Dublin hostelry, The Hay Hotel, with virtues that constituted a Hegelian dialectic with its vices.

> There is a window stuffed with hay
> Like herbage in an oven cast;
> And there we came at break of day
> To soothe ourselves with light repast:
> And men who worked before the mast,
> And drunken girls delectable—
> A future symbol of our past
> You'll maybe, find the Hay Hotel.

Tumbling in the Hay was an immediate success. Reviewing it, Harold Nicolson referred to the difficulty of re-creating with words an illusion of life's dynamic fantasy. This had been achieved by Smollett and Fielding and now by Gogarty in a book which had immense humanity, and, however much it might cause readers to laugh, was a work of very competent art. Despite wartime restrictions it went into a second edition. But by then its author was in America.

5

O My America!

A comparison of Gogarty with Gauguin could not be sustained beyond the similarity of their throwing up good positions at the dictates of the Muses. Gogarty chose no tropical paradise but what is merely Magna Graecia for the Irish, and unlike Gaugin his best work was already done. The Dublin family, nevertheless, even though the children were grown, must have experienced a sense of upheaval when the father turned his back on a remunerative practice. In those days Dublin doctors did not retire: Gogarty's exceptional action came in the sour aftermath of the libel cases, and of the deaths of so many friends—"Nor, after Caesar, skulk in Rome"—and in a phase of political disillusionment, the ex-Senator at odds with the party in power. But the strongest motive was the long-submerged conflict between the frustrated artist and the reluctant clinician which was resolved in the liberation of the former. Too late, alas! For he was in his sixties; his enshackled creativeness experienced no resurgence when professional cares were abandoned.

His optimistic temperament responded to his new environment. "In Europe things are referred back. In America they are referred to a future in which every man has sublime confidence." Its landscapes had an unaccustomed spaciousness: "Of trees in bloom, who can speak? Acre after acre of apple orchard in bloom—a sight that can hardly be sustained, such is the joy it transmits" —best revealed from the air. The novelty of air travel, difficult for present-day readers to appreciate, is well expressed in a poem "Over Ohio" which tells us how he can behold East and West, godlike, in a glance and

See alternate valleys gleam
Each one with its little stream,
And the undulant, immense,
Free, American expanse.

The apotheosis of the urban is realized in New York City, and Gogarty was astounded by the beauty of Manhattan. "When I see the moon hung low between the magic towers of the city, I am spellbound. Nowhere is there such a sight as the electric lights in the countless skyey windows multiplied against the clear calmness of the southern sky."

He was impressed by the intellignece of the women he met and by their potentiality for counteracting oppression and cruelty. "Woman has denuded herself of mystery. She has become contemptuous of her pedestal. She has descended into the arena with man. . . The position of women in the United States is the best augury for its future."

From his apartment in the Ritz Tower on Park

Avenue at Fifty-seventh Street he wrote to William
Lyon Phelps of Yale on September 9, 1940, and mentioned future plans: "I have sold two books to Lippin-
cott and as one deals with Kentucky I have decided to
remain on until October 14th and 6 months after that if
I can get an extension of visa. I tried to join up in
Canada but they found out my age as if it mattered to
me any more than Time touches you."

He obtained the necessary permit and eventually he
became an American citizen. In his mocking way he
called Ireland "a place or state of punishment where
some souls suffer until the time comes when they can go
abroad." When questioned as to his intention of return-
ing there he would say, "Why should I? In Dublin I'd
spend most of my time sitting in pubs talking to people
for nothing. Here I make a comfortable living saying the
same thing for money." But in another mood the exile
would affirm his intention of finally going home.

Among his new friends was a Dr. Spickers with
whom he stayed at Wyckoff, New Jersey, or at the
Spickers' summer house on Barnegat Bay. "I owe him
much," Gogarty wrote. "When with him I felt myself in
the shelter of a soul at peace." His elegy in *Perennial* for
his host's son Albert, who died in a plane crash, was an
act of piety which did not come off, but the sympa-
thetic essay "William Spickers, M.D." in the post-
humously published *A Weekend in the Middle of the
Week* is devoid of flippancy and makes one wish that
Gogarty had written more often in this vein instead of
striving so continuously to uphold his reputation as a
wit. Addressing his friend in Wyckoff at a time when life
in Manhattan was no longer a novelty, Gogarty recov-

ered his lyric flair in a sonnet echoing Yeats at Coole Park:

> You like the country better than the town
> And very willingly would dwell therein
> Afar from the intolerable din
> That makes New York a barbarous Babylon;
> But far more willingly would I be gone
> From all this mad bombardment of the brain
> To fields where still and comely thoughts may reign
> Deep in your stately mansion old and brown,
> And coloured like a Springtime copper beech:
> My God I would give anything to reach
> Your old house standing in the misty rain,
> And turn my thoughts to things that do not pass,
> While gazing through a window at the grass
> And wet young oak leaves fingering the pane.

Gideon Ousley makes a reappearance in *Going Native*, in which the author describes his surrogate's fictional experiences in English country houses. The humor in this book borders on burlesque; it satirizes English moods and manners and compares English and Irish attitudes. "There is no Kingdom of Heaven over here; the British Empire has replaced it."

The very names of the people we encounter—Snaith, Snape and Treblecock are of the servants' hall, Sir Chalfont St. Gules very upper-crust—are parodies of social polarization. The characterization is unconvincing; readers may find it difficult to become involved and especially those who cut their teeth on *Couples* or *Last Exit to Brooklyn*. Ousley's comic bedroom encounters—"I to be jilted by a Vicar's niece. It took fifty women to cool Cuchulian from his battle fury."—would have made Fresh Nelly despair of him.

The English have always made "victory out of defeat. The Conquest is a feather in their caps. They have everything both ways." Ousley loses patience with them and recalls the thrushes singing in Glenasmole. Finally he asks himself ". . .how long can I abide this civilization, the greatest civilization on earth? How long can I live with the pirates who put on dinner jackets?"

The best in *Going Native*, and as usual Gogarty excels in descriptive writing, is the art of the essayist and not that of a novelist:

> I was hard at work getting myself reconciled to the pollarding of the willows, to me another reminder of the orderly hand which is at work over the whole country and has been at work from time immemorial bringing all things, even the landscape, within the law; and thinking how different are the black and sour sally trees which grow in Connemara of the little lakes and flourish solitarily upright and untamed on the central island which nearly every lake possesses. Black, sour, choppy willow trees, good for a heronry or to shelter the red-berried mountain ash. . . .

But versatile to a fault Gogarty was not deterred from a still more ambitious undertaking, historical fiction.

Mad Grandeur is a romance set in 1798, a year of rebellion. This is a long book and Gogarty's tale of the fortunes of Hyacinth Martyn-Lynch and his bride is set against a detailed background of eighteenth-century Irish life when the existence of gaming, dueling landlords was in dramatic contrast to the plight of an oppressed peasantry. Highwaymen, pugilists, racing touts, including an engaging rascal. Toucher Plant, and the Bucks of the Hell Fire Club, provide additional color.

"Yeats has begun to evict imaginary tenants!"

Gogarty joked about his friend's tendency to identify himself with the landed gentry but made no secret of the fact that he, too, loved a lord. The Big Houses in *Mad Grandeur* are composites of Lady Gregory's Coole Park, Edward Martyn's Tulira, Moore Hall, and the Gore-Booth's Lissadell. Gogarty's hero, Martyn-Lynch, is a County Mayo landlord and doubtless his warning by d'Estournelles, a French emigré, reechoes the author's personal sentiments:

> "As one who has some experience of the *canaille* in revolt, I know that it is not so much their wrongs that makes them destructive at the very sight of culture and refinement. Perhaps these are associated in their minds with superiority and aristocracy, and I suppose to some extent they always will be," he said with some slight sarcasm: adding, "It is advisable to put one's pictures and silver out of the way when one goes to the aid of the People."

Many treasured possessions and irreplaceable paintings perished in the flames of Renvyle House. Yet Gogarty and his Anglo-Irish landlords Martyn-Lynch and Denis St. George knew where the ultimate blame lay for Ireland's long history of political unrest. "The English Government has destroyed the shipping and wool trade of this country, part of the revenue of which goes to Dublin Castle to corrupt the politicians of the Irish Parliament. As far as I can see it will end with the suppression of the Irish Parliament and the rigging up of a union with the English constitution."

French troops landed in Killala in August 1798. The English fled before them at their first engagement, "the Races of Castlebar," but this victory was not repeated. Martyn-Lynch and his like were accused of disloyalty by the English and their houses sacked by their tenants.

For men of spirit nothing remained but to build new lives in Virginia.

Others followed their example, and in *Mr. Petunia,* a novel based on the misadventures of a paranoid watchmaker, Toucher Plant, despite a new dignity conferred by prosperity, remains true to his nature. When the right moment arrives he contrives to dispose of a barren mare to an overtrusting customer.

During his own years in America Gogarty contributed to a number of magazines, and like others obliged to live by their pens he discovered that what has been sold once can be sold twice, or, indeed, many times. *Mourning Became Mrs. Spendlove* (1948) contains stories (the title is taken from a tall tale about a courtesan) and essays. Unfortunately the former show the short story as an art form in which Gogarty did not excel; the best essay was "Reminiscences of Yeats." "Dublin Revisited" I and II describe a visit to his native city—"Back to my unfriendly, friendly, bitter Ithaca"—after six years' absence. These essays of a returned exile were expanded, after a second visit to Ireland, in *Rolling Down the Lea* (1950), which is a eulogy of Dublin with reservations, and a Connemara rhapsody.

It is springtime in Dublin—"one of the most beautiful cities in Europe, with its five squares, its domes and the Palladian architecture of its public edifices"—and its people are smiling. We meet some of them: Mac-Glornan, a small-time politician; Richard Best, the scholar; Jack Nugent, mine host of the famous Dolphin Hotel; and Dulcie, "a lady pink and white" who despite her wayward youth had one thing in common with the saints, *fragrance.* "Dulcie diffuses fragrance. She is the only one I ever met who did."

Behind the splendor of the spring our guide discerns human failings; "Meanness, chicanery and self-interest all were there"—just as in Athens. But Gogarty's saving grace is to remember that he himself is "part of the show"; to preserve his sense of the ridiculous, "a precious and salutary gift"; and to be aware of his own astringency in a town where friendliness may veil malevolence.

He rails against the slums as he did in *Blight*. "Those born in slums have a slum outlook. They have been deprived of beauty." But perhaps not completely. The delights of the Georgian masonry have not been completely effaced in their role of tenements: ". . .the rose-red shadows they cast in the twilight bring back the purple splendour of the prime."

For the city's shortcomings he hurls scorn upon the politicians.

> Those in authority would seem to have joined the conspiracy against the light. We see them dressed in black hats and dark broadcloth, as if they would put out the light of day. Their pomp is as fallacious as the marble in the movie-halls of O'Connell Street and, worse than all, they know not what they do. They have blighted life for the people. Will these blighters never laugh?

His particular detestation of de Valera (he looks "like a laugh in mourning") has already erupted in "Dublin Revisited"—"this impersonation of casuistry, hypocrisy and humbug"—and needs no further mention.

Dublin is surrounded by race courses and Gogarty takes us to one of them passing through tinkers, pedlars and fortune-tellers into the enclosure to join "pink Englishmen, brown foreigners; fat women who were not

homebred, and the usual lank hunting-women whom we
all knew, and the hurried, busy long-nosed men," and to
watch the bookies on their stands "shouting like muez-
zins." And then surprisingly—or perhaps not, for
Gogarty's melancholy has already been noted—watching
the bobbing sea of heads, he reflects: "A few years, and
they all shall have disappeared like clouds that cross a
hill."

When the clouds have crossed the sun reappears. Soon
we are on a west-bound train and after Athlone come to

> Ballinasloe, where the hostings were
> Ballinasloe, of the great horse-fair
> That gathers in horses from Galway and Clare.
> Wherever the fields of limestone are:
> Mayo and Boyle and Coolavin
> Between the miles of rushes and whin. . . .

and so to Galway and Connemara.

> The wonder of this many-coloured land lies in the change
> of colours, which are never for an hour the same shade. To
> name them in a language that has hardly a dozen names for
> colour would be impossible. Plum-blue, hyacinth, cyclamen
> and every flower that grows in the country would have to
> be enlisted, and then they would never give the impression
> of living and glowing hues. The mountain lakes are more
> than black; the mountains are lapis lazuli mixed with velvet
> brown; sea inlets take on shades that no words can name.

At that time Renvyle House had passed to other
hands but the Gogartys owned a house on Freilaun
(Heather Island) in Tully Lake. The endless peace of this
beautiful region must have been in startling contrast to
the ceaseless noise of Manhattan which Gogarty had so
recently left. But there was a drawback, heavy rainfall.

"Were it not for the clouds off the Atlantic that bring in rain, I would never leave Renvyle with its glimmering islands and its assured faith in wonders of the deep."

The autobiographical *It Isn't this Time of Year at All*! is a discursive anecdotal account of life in Dublin and elsewhere somewhat carelessly written—the story of Sir Thornley Stoker and Lord Dunsany's butler is repeated within a few pages—in conversational style. This is a defect of Gogarty's later books: the eye of the reader scanning lines of prose has to imagine the quizzical smile that accompanied the telling, but when the hesitations and shifting tones of a matchless raconteur are missing it sometimes falls flat. And if individually published essays are not delicately pruned when collected the recurrence of certain expressions and phrases robs them of freshness.

Horace Reynolds, a generous eulogist of Gogarty, knew his shortcomings: "Gogarty wrote as a tiger hunts: if he missed his spring he would not try again, and this refusal to recognise the work in writing meant that some of what he wrote was mechanical and disconnected. But there were always days when he did not miss his target."

The egoism of advancing years, pardonable and easy to circumvent in conversation but ineradicable on the printed page, was an added defect especially when superimposed on a natural assertiveness. His mind was closed to new ideas in art. He described paintings in an Exhibition of Living Art as "illustrations for the dermatology of a leper colony." He disparaged modern poets: "Poetry is courage and theirs is the opposite." His dislike of psychoanalysis overflowed into his verse.

The growing interest and perceptive analysis in America of the works of James Joyce irritated him increasingly.

The relationship of the former friends has been considered in detail in the present author's *James Joyce and Medicine* and discussion here is avoided beyond the comment that Gogarty gave more to Joyce intellectually, materially, and in affection than he received from him; but it is germane to say that Gogarty's ill-advised "They Think They Know Joyce" had a boomerang effect, shattering his own credibility. It is urged that those who wish to come to an objective appraisal of Gogarty should set aside the dialogue of disparagement in which he and Joyce engaged and also his dehumanizing characterization as Buck Mulligan in *Ulysses.*

A hospital colleague said that Gogarty was "a first-class writer, a second-class patriot, and a third-class surgeon." The literary pundits of today would reverse the order and the patriots (in Ireland we have patriots rather than citizens) might tell a still different story.

Terence de Vere White recently observed that "Wilde had whatever genius is; Gogarty only walked in its shadow." But surely this Dublin vice of denigratory comparison is a futile exercise recalling Swift's "smaller fleas that on him prey." Literary judgments use for measurement the variable scale of human affect and are often reversed on appeal. Literary assessments stand on the quicksands of fashion, open to the pull of subconscious prejudice. Besides, the present-day trend to let the books make the tally, scoring nothing for their creators' apparently unrelated virtues, subtracting nothing for their gaucheries and limitations, is a trend that favors the colorless and the single-minded but improverishes literary history.

Let us, then, before we see him off the stage, spare a moment to look once more at Gogarty in the round: it is not enough to credit him, at the minimum, with some consummate lyrics and that comic masterpiece *Tumbling in the Hay*; we must remember and proclaim those qualities which made him equally at ease with the dons in the common room and with the hearties on the playing fields, that allowed him to walk with assurance into an operating room, a tavern, or a drawing room. He moved in a group where wit was the common currency, the tokens minted as often as not in fires of malice; the recollection of his verbal incontinence must be balanced by the indubitable fact of his gift for friendship. And what friends he had!

It is inappropriate to say that he squandered his talents without conceding how right he was to decide that life was to be lived. A man of Gogarty's versatility offends mediocrity. Rather than leave it to any of Dublin's grudging critics to say the last word, let a former British poet laureate, William Watson, do so:

> Three Olivers before you time
> Were not unknown in prose and rhyme;
> One was the paladin or pal
> Of him who fought at Roncesvalles,
> And one brought Drogheda to pillage
> And one wrote "The Deserted Village";
> But sorra an Oliver ever seen
> Compares with him of Stephen's Green.

One has the impression that towards the end his ebullience was replaced by bitterness, and that behind the bravado of those last years in exile lay unhappiness. Like every author he had disappointments. The typescript of "Oddities" was turned down by the Abelard

Press in June 1952. (It was later published as *A Week-end in the Middle of the Week*.) His projected *Nine Worthies* was not completed; the essay on Yeats was published by Dublin's Dolmen Press in 1963, those on A.E. and James Stephens appeared in the *Colby Library Quarterly* in May 1955 and March 1961 respectively. Mary Manning, who thought that of all the Irish Renaissance group he was the most human, the most endearing, knew him at this period and saw him as a lonely man, hard-up and drifting around New York. "Someone from Dublin would enter the room, the sadness would vanish, the face light up and out would come a stream of beautiful talk." But the golden days were long since gone, and the last of Oliver Gogarty's books published in his lifetime concludes with the characteristic admonition, "Let us laugh while we may, for in the end we shall all have to walk off the big plank into the dark stuff. . ." A heart attack in Manhattan took him to the start of that short journey on September 19, 1957. When he died three days later in the Beth Israel Hospital, his remains were flown to Shannon for burial in the peace of Connemara where his gravestone in Ballinakill cemetery is inscribed with lines from "Non Dolet":

> Our friends go with us as we go
>   Down the long path where Beauty wends
> Where all we love forgathers, so
>   Why should we fear to join our friends?

Selected Bibliography

1. WORKS BY OLIVER ST. JOHN GOGARTY

Prose

As I Was Going Down Sackville Street. London, 1937, 1954, 1968; New York, 1937.
I Follow Saint Patrick. London and New York, 1938.
Tumbling in the Hay. London and New York, 1939.
Going Native. New York, 1940; London, 1941.
Mad Grandeur. Philadelphia, 1941; London, 1943.
Mr. Petunia. New York, 1945; London, 1946.
Mourning Became Mrs. Spendlove. New York, 1948.
Rolling Down The Lea. London, 1950.
Intimations. New York, 1950.
It Isn't that Time of Year at All. London and New York, 1954.
Start from Somewhere Else. New York, 1955.
A Weekend in the Middle of the Week and Other Essays on the Bias. New York, 1958.
W. B. Yeats: A Memoir. Dublin, 1963.

Poetry

Hyperthuleana. Dublin, 1916.
The Ship and Other Poems. Dublin, 1918.
An Offering of Swans. Dublin, 1923, 1971.

An Offering of Swans and Other Poems. London, 1924.
Wild Apples. Dublin, 1928, 1971; New York, 1929.
Wild Apples: with a preface by W. B. Yeats. Dublin, 1930, 1971.
Selected Poems. New York, 1933.
Others to Adorn. London, 1938.
Elbow Room. Dublin, 1939; New York, 1942.
Perennial. Baltimore, 1944; London, 1946.
The Collected Poems. New York, 1950; London, 1951.
Unselected Poems. Baltimore, 1954.

Plays

Blight. Dublin, 1917.
A Serious Thing. Dublin, 1919.
The Enchanted Trousers. Dublin, 1919.
The Plays of Oliver St. John Gogarty. Edited by James F. Carens. Newark, 1971.

Letters

Many Lines to Thee. Edited by James F. Carens. Dublin, 1971.

2. SECONDARY STUDIES

Carens, James F. "Joyce and Gogarty." *New Light on Joyce from the Dublin Symposium*. Edited by F. Senn. Indiana, 1973.
–––. "Gogarty and Yeats" in *Modern Irish Literature*. Edited by Porter, R. J. and Brophy, J. D. New York, 1972.
The Catholic Bulletin 14 (1923): 5-7; 23 (1923): 327-31.
Doolin, William. Obituary Notice. *The Lancet*, October 5, 1957.
Fanning, Stephen. *The Kilkenny Magazine* (Autumn/Winter 1963), p. 10.
Fitzwilliam, Michael (pseudonym of J. B. Lyons).

"Gogarty, Doctor and Writer." *Medical News*, June 21, 1963.

Gogarty, Oliver D. "My Brother Willie Was Your Father's Friend." *Bibliotheca Bucnellensis* 7 (1969): 1-13.

Griffin, Gerald. *The Wild Geese*. London, 1938.

Jeffares, A. Norman. *Proceedings of the British Academy* 46: 73-98.

–––. *The Circus Animals*. London, 1970.

Kain, Richard. *Dublin in the Age of Joyce and Yeats*.

Lyons J. B. *James Joyce and Medicine*. Dublin, 1973.

–––. "Irish Doctors and Literature." *Dublin Magazine* (Autumn/Winter 1973/74).

Mercier, Vivian. *The Irish Comic Tradition*. Oxford, 1962.

–––. *Poetry* 93, no. 1 (1958): 35-40.

M. N. C. "Arch-Mocker." *Ireland To-Day* (May 1937), pp. 80-81.

Myles na Gopaleen. *Irish Times*, September 25, 1957.

O'Connor, Frank. *My Father's Son*. Dublin, 1968.

O'Connor, Ulick. *The Times I've Seen–Oliver St. John Gogarty*. New York, 1963.

Rogers, W. R., ed. *Irish Literary Portraits*. London, 1972.

Smith, Grover. "Yeats, Gogarty, and the Leap Castle Ghost," in *Modern Irish Literature*. Edited by Porter, R. J. and Brophy, J. D. New York, 1972.

Times Literary Supplement, July, 21, 1972.

White, Terence de V. *The Anglo-Irish*. London, 1972.

Wilson, T. G. "Oliver St. John Gogarty, M.D. F.R.C.S.I." *Archives of Otolaryngology* (August 1969) pp. 235-43.